Love Is A Mountain

Love Is A Mountain

Mozella

Perry

Ademiluyi

© Copyright 2009 Mozella Perry Ademiluyi All Rights Reserved

No part of this book may be used or reproduced by any means, graphic, electronic, or mechanical, including photocopying, recording, taping, or by any information retrieval system without the express written permission of the author except in the case of brief quotations embodied in critical articles and reviews.

ISBN: 978-0-9819644-0-9

Love Is A Mountain, LLC
4800 Hampden Lane
Suite 200
Bethesda, MD 20814

www.loveisamountain.com

Logo design: ScreenTint
www.ScreenTint.com

Printed in the United States of America

Choreography

In Gratitude, *ix*

Love is

- Beginnings, 15
- Flight, 19
- Being, 22
- Friendship, 24
- Today, 27
- Magic, 29
- Bridges, 32
- Coloured Girl, 35
- Taj Mahal, 39
- Canyons, 42
- A Bag of Coffee Beans, 45
- I want to know, 49

- Alone, 53
- Pitons, 56
- Knock, Knock, 59
- Longing, 62
- Love Letter, 67
- How Do I Hold You, 69
- Moon Rocks, 72
- Together, 75
- Gratitude Whispers, 78
- You, 80
- Night & Day, 82
- Another Horizon, 85
- A Master of Disguise, 88
- Sacred Ties, 91
- Stars at Life, 93
- Autumn…time…, 95
- Beyond, 98
- The Mirror Holders, 101
- The Gift, 106
- Love Is a Mountain, 108

A Mountain

- Mount Kilimanjaro, 113

About the author, 121

In Gratitude

Many hands have lovingly touched my life and this, my first book project. Many hearts have expressed encouragement.

Thank you Adegboyega for saying yes to all I've wished to embark upon...the sane and seemingly insane desires I've had.

Thank you June Michael and Gboyega Ademola (NYC) for the tremendous parts you have played: for helping me recognize and acknowledge a God given gift of expression – and the courage to share it. June, I appreciate your invaluable guidance and structure. And Gboyega, your amazing body of knowledge and instruction taught me loads and lit the way to press.

To my boys with loads of love: Yemi, William, Seyi, Toks and the very special others who call me Mom.

To my friends who helped me say "yes" to myself: Chu Chu, Diane, Jon and Nancy and to many others held in heart and mind as we crisscrossed each other's paths.

For Marie Onwuachi who said "call me any time of day or night"...and willingly helped me with the daunting tasks of 'fixing it' so that even I could read it.

Changamiré and Lincoln Ross for their audio artistry in creating the CD of selected poems from this book. And you Changamiré for overseeing the entire project.

Thank you Nature: the sun, moon and her stars. Thank you to my nights and my days.

And I honor my late parents, Moses and Johnnie Perry, who gave us untold numbers of gifts, adventures, Africa, the deepest friendships and experiences one could ever hope for in a lifetime.....for Kat, Shirley and Moses, Jr. who walked the 'safari' with me.

Most of all, thank you God for choices; for the power of the spoken word; for love and mountains.

Mozella Perry Ademiluyi

June 1, 2009

In loving memory of my parents,
Moses and Johnnie Perry,
who infused my world with light,
love and many brilliant colors.

Love Is

BEGINNINGS

I attended elementary school in Jinja, Uganda, junior high school in Eldoret, Kenya and graduated from high school in Kijabe, Kenya.

I always begin in 1962 when I was nine years old. That year marked a dramatic shift in my life.

It all started with my father and his dreams. During high school and on through college years, he formed a deep desire to live and work in Africa. He had worked for the local YMCA for over a decade, and said yes to an opportunity, both a call and an answer, to begin an international YMCA in East Africa, with a focus and goals around youth leadership and vocational development.

I admire his courage and forward thinking. He bundled his entire family up: wife, son, three daughters and moved us from Miami, Florida to Jinja, Uganda in October 1962. He left behind the important era of the civil rights movements in the States and forged fully into the emerging independent continent of Africa. These were significant times on both sides of the world.

My parents recalled how there was a deep concern amongst their family and friends that they were taking these young children to the "dark continent" as the unknown African continent was called in those days. I still marvel at my parents' leap of faith. They shared and acted on a vision that expanded well beyond anything in our immediate, Miami-based environment.

Our journey to East Africa was an adventure in itself. Our video camera, a bon voyage gift, provided the perfect "moving album," capturing so much of our historic journey. As a family, we had never left the country before. From the States we flew to Monrovia, Liberia, then to Accra, Ghana, on to Addis Ababa, Ethiopia, Nairobi, Kenya and then into Kampala, Uganda—each stay an acclimatizing step representing yet another level of our newly found cultural experience.

In Uganda, my world opened to the many gifts different peoples of the world bring. My sisters and I, and a handful of Ugandan and Asian families, were amongst the first to integrate Victoria Nile School, the newly renamed, post-colonial British primary school we attended.

Over the years that followed, our parents encouraged us to immerse ourselves in the exquisite beauty and opportunities offered by our richly textured environment.

Tons of stories weave their way through my life growing up in East Africa. From it all, I developed a passion for people, their cultures and our Earth's beauty which, in my opinion, is especially splendid in that part of the world.

Our experiences and travel multiplied — every three years we would return to the States for brief summer visits. En route, we often participated in enriching exploratory and conference stays in other parts of the world.

Each return visit to the States demonstrated how different we had become from the other kids our age who were awed that we lived in "Africa" (said in a big, yet hushed way). "Do you sleep in a house; do you swing from trees?" At that time, most Americans were largely unaware of life outside their own shores.

In the years when there was no "home leave," our holidays took us into the hinterlands and landscapes of Uganda. They also took us across borders to more expeditions in other parts of East Africa including the coastal areas, Kenya's exquisite tidal reef, and the foot of Mt. Kilimanjaro in Moshi, Tanzania. The Masai herdsmen amazed me.

I remember the fear as an alarmed elephant charged us during a safari; my father making a panicked reverse along the dirt road, my brother seated beside him adeptly videotaping the whole episode.

I wondered at the strength of women who had babies on their backs and tall, heavy loads on their heads whilst taking erect strides to who-knew-where. My sisters and I marveled at the sight of a single family on one bicycle and vowed to try it out as soon as we made it back home.

If we seemed not to notice something, our parents brought it to our attention. "Look over there, how many colors of green can you see?" my dad would say to keep us occupied during a long road journey.

With all this came a greater appreciation of adventure, people, tradition, land, and an unknown energy which moved throughout it all. Ugandans, British, other Europeans, Africans from other nations and Asians added greater depth and flavor to all that we were learning, tasting and absorbing. It was an unimaginably rich, full, and uniquely exciting time for a young African American girl. In my life, friendships of all kinds have deep international roots.

In recent years, I have the continued fortune of rediscovering and renewing childhood friendships borne out of our years in East Africa. It has been magical to share memories with people who were there for some of my most significant, developmental experiences. These friends are living testaments and open memory banks to the many stories we have travelled along together.

Those nine years stirred the vessels of poetry within me and influenced everything else that has followed. They inspired the knowing I sensed before the majestic Victoria Falls in Zimbabwe and the luminous Taj Mahal in India; just as they drew sacred murmurings from my breath at first sights of the Grand Canyon in Arizona. The impact of those years took my sisters and I back to climb the famed rooftops of Mt. Kilimanjaro for my fiftieth birthday.

I have the deepest gratitude for Life, for Love, for Mountains.

Flight

clouds cast lonely shadows

on cracked barren land

on and on as far

as eyes could see:

reflections of despair

left behind, an expanse

of undulating snow capped

peaks,

beautiful:

frozen possibilities

ahead, ahead lies hope

in lush green,

rich savannahs

life

and nature:

intertwined places of

consciousness

and above it all,

a sky filled with

limitless probabilities

regardless of what

lies below:

and my soul sings...

February 6, 2003

I felt these words at an altitude of roughly 35,000 feet. What a sight to travel from Europe down into Africa. I had seen it time and again, yet I just could not stop taking in the breathtaking views from the oval frame of my window.

Life can change ever so quickly. We move from one space to another in such relatively short periods. We take it all in, it affects us — and then it's over—that is, unless we have a way to harness the memory. Writing does that, pictures do that, and so does sharing stories.

Being

place your understanding

behind 'that'

and see light

beneath darkness

sound

beyond the silence

hear a touch

and feel what you heard

know your search

is over

and that right

where you are is

where you

need to be

March 8, 2003

When I was a child in Uganda, our "shamba boy"—the nameless colonial terminology for gardeners—told me a tree had spoken to him. I believed him. Later, when I was an adult in Nigeria, our house steward declared he could "hear the smell." Perhaps he made a grammatical slip, and yet, in some strange way, I believed that he "heard" a smell.

Living around people who either operated or expressed themselves outside western norms was a powerful influence. I never forgot either one of those seemingly unrelated statements, and many others like them. It taught me to pay more attention to subtle energies, parables and the unexpected.

Friendship

deep within your eyes

we've journeyed together

on paths only you had walked

showing me along life's rivers,

life's banks

deep within your eyes

light flickered an eternal

beacon to follow...

never did we lose our way

even when darkness

hovered around us

deep within your eyes

pain was erased

by soothing treasures

of joy, love

understanding,

compassion...

we paused...

at peace

we savored their goodness

deep within your eyes,

you tell me our paths

will cross again...

somewhere...

deep within your eyes

May 2, 2002

Friendships are true wealth.

What a wonderful period in my life to be reconnected with friends from Victoria Nile School, Loreto Convent and Rift Valley Academy—all schools I attended in Uganda and Kenya. The chances seemed so slim for decades. Then, one by one, so many are arriving back into my life, reminding us all of so much adventure: long train rides to boarding schools; journeys around craters in the great Rift Valley; and stories from a diverse group of youth connected by powerful African threads.

Today

greeting our sun...

bathing in the warmth

of her golden rays

I drink crisp morning air

like deeply satisfying

sips of wine

each part of me

tingles

with life

and love

in motion

today

I live for

today

because

tomorrow

I...

November 7, 2003

Magic

A giant of a man, possessed

of many talents

gentleness and healing energy

emanate from his hands

wisest of words flow from his lips

like liquid gold...

and, he gives away love and

compassion through his eyes

a mystic of a man is he...

great depths of knowledge

reside in many hidden places

oh that he would see himself

through the inside of his own vision

and awaken to the magic of

his own soul

June 18, 2004

It's not unusual for people not to 'see' themselves. And it is such a gift to reflect their own beauty and sheer genius back to them.

Who was it that said, "Man know thyself!" What a huge command. We will search high and low, move from one relationship to another, one job here, the next one there — searching and looking for something or someone outside of ourselves who will make us happy and whole.

It is right there all along. The very place we're most afraid to look. What a journey it requires: such feats and courage to be still, go inside, and find our heart's desires. Our needs are often met within the hidden treasures of our very own mind and thoughts.

It's just too simplistic and, therefore, much too hard to accept.

Map out what we want...? What a 'blasphemous' idea...and yet...it's the same story preached in all sacred texts...the same approach proclaimed by both old and modern day sages, authors and gurus...they all...keep saying...the same thing...over and over again...

Oh, to awaken to the magic of our souls!

Bridges

you are

a

bridge

across the waters

connecting

me and

my other self

water mirrors

reflect

my sense of self,

smiling lovingly,

encouraging and

coaxing me to

life's higher ground

"you can do it"

they gurgle

in response

to my unspoken questions,

"follow your heart"

murmurs the babbling brook

because of you

i hear the sounds

of my own footsteps

in sync with

nature's harmonic tones

because

of you

i feel the solidity

beneath my feet

...stable, earthy

and strong...

February 11, 2005

Coloured Girl

the radiance of the sun filters

through her aura

coloring the spaces

through which she walks

like an angel she moves...

heads turn though they know not why

for her power is felt, not seen...

her message is

perceived, not heard...

blues, palest fuchsia

and lavender hues pulsate

from her shoulders,

extending over her head

cascading down,

around and out from her body...

truly she is the one

for whom we wait

she is the 'he'

another messenger of God

a coloured girl...

a coloured girl has come

to save us

from the black and white

of our colorless selves

she walks with us,

amongst us...for us...

will we reject her

like the hims who came before

or will we open our hearts,

our closed minds

and receive the rainbow of her gifts,

her love...

do you see

that coloured girl...

simple...but...

She is...

You are...

and I am

...a coloured girl....

October 16, 2003

Taj Mahal

how majestic...his love...so white, so pure, so deep

how tenderly he detailed

the memory of her body,

her soul

and the beauty of her spirit...

soft, illumined by light, by color

oh we long for love...

his love,

her love

their love...our love

wrapped in joy and a wonderful mystique

he waits for her,

anticipating her return...

he waits

and he waits

and his love grows bigger than life

magnificent promises fulfilled

in holy submission he lets go

she rests...he rests

we rest in love

November 18, 2001

Seeing the Taj Mahal was like a dream come true. Yes, the pictures I've seen of it have been amazing; however, seeing it for myself was an exquisite treat. I went to India with Amber, my childhood friend from Uganda, just months after September 11th – a time when many people, understandably, were deathly afraid to travel. So it was a quiet time all over the world, a palpable, fearful hush.

Like all the rooms in the magnificent Amarvilas at Agra, our room faced the Taj. So, in the morning, as soon as the mist lifted, there she was—calling from a distance. When we visited later that morning and went through the gates, I gasped, it was huge. For a moment, it was as if I'd died and gone to heaven!

This poetic memory reflects the story behind the Taj. It is a deep love story carrying a lot of pride, pain, and death for those who built what I believe to be one of the most intricate of all man-made monuments.

You leave the Taj with yet another view of what love looks and feels like—of what it can produce.

Canyons

magnificent temples,

ancient carved cities filled

with stories created

many, many

millions of years ago

our eyes roam the depth and

splendor of nature's

sunken treasures

the grandest of canyons...

home of the gods themselves

we wonder

and whisper in reverence

and disbelief...

awed by the Forces

which call this place home

we stand there like tiny specks

in the minutest of seconds

contemplating eons gone by

knowing that when we leave

this place, it remains

for yet another eternity

and that we have left our prayers

in the midst of forever...

August 9, 2004

Soaking in the Grand Canyon was another one of those great gasping moments for me. It felt like the same awe I experienced standing before Victoria Falls in Zimbabwe, or Uganda's Rwenzori Mountain Range.

"Magnificent architecture" inadequately describes the astoundingly beautiful, natural treasures of our earth.

A Bag of Coffee Beans

it doesn't take much

to express care,

send love

or create

a memory flood...

a bag of beans will do

i held it in my space

infusing the aroma

and taste of me

our hands,

mine

and then yours

will have embraced

without touching,

our eyes will have seen

—separated—

yet not apart

for I placed an ounce of love

for every bean contained

in this burlap mask

...waiting its turn to drip through

and finally be savored

by your lips

heart ventures far

when it cannot be direct,

but, it always,

always

finds its way

...and so, without a

spoken

or written word

I sent you a bag of beans...

I sent you love

April 11, 2006

Gifts, love and appreciation come in all kinds of packages. Try passing up the department store versions and simply ask your heart: "how do I express this?"

Whether it's a small gift with a huge message or a big gift with a short and sweet one; the answers to it all lie in the question.

Most people do not write letters anymore. Hand-written letters and cards can convey so much more to the senses, much, much more than a box of Godiva chocolates or the roses. Our letters shared what today's text messages can't. Go to the stationery store, sit with your heart and let it flow…what a gift to even you, the giver.

I Want To Know

I want to hear what

we see when we look

through each other's eyes

searching,

reading...understanding

I want to hear

I want to identify

what's behind the intensity

of our touch

the breathless fullness

resonating above our merged souls

I long to know the name

of the space we fill with

each other

if it has a name

I want to know

how deep is deep

how long is long...

I want to know

your thoughts,

the ones unsaid,

the ones

about to be,

waiting to be

expressed...

Tell me where you want to go

and how far

you're willing

to walk

And if I can walk

along beside you

for a while

I want to know

August 1, 2004

Poetry longs to be read aloud. In my childhood, we were required to read volumes of great works, memorize and recite important passages. Reading the work of others often generates response. David Whyte's poem, 'Self-Portrait', influenced I Want To Know. Other writers can subtly invite you to pose your own questions, to dig deeper and understand more than the obvious. We move beyond the surface to the real meaning of what we feel, see, and touch when we claim love. We long to know where 'the other' is in his or her process.

Alone

Alone:

by candle light

I watched silhouettes

slowly disappear

into the night's

embracing air…

exquisite birds

of paradise

against a madras

laden table…

sipping wine...

dipping in and out of

surrounding conversations...

Alone:

feeling

serene, peaceful

and quite content

to just "be"

Alone:

enjoying

the romance

of it all...

July 9, 2004

I was at the stunningly beautiful Ladera Resort in St. Lucia having dinner, alone, watching the Pitons – two spectacular volcanic mountains — fade away into the night.

I stayed in one of their "tree house" rooms with only three walls — a true adventure for those who choose to ignore the creepy, crawly possibilities and instead drink in the open-air view of a lush green mountainside.

Beyond the canopy of my mosquito net, creatures were busily singing their night lives away. They played an uncanny symphony of sound and movement.

And I heard myself say out loud: "Did you hear that?!!!" And alone…replied, "Yes…did you?"

Pitons

under a clearly blue sky

I 'flew slowly' along the ocean waves

bouncing gently, reclined

watching a soaring seagull...

and the wisps of white floating above...

nature's feasts, at sea,

soaking

in magnificence...

---pitons---

protruding proudly from the ocean's chest

like emerging treasures bursting

into receptive space

rocks, cliffs all placed along

this jagged puzzle

of perfection...

celebrating life!

as the sun dips lower

drinking,

drinking

almost gone...

slipping below

a glaze, a glow...
a glorious day!

July, 2003

A description of the motor boat ride to the Pitons is one thing, climbing them is quite another! I just had to experience the Gros Piton, the easier and larger of the two volcanic mountains in beautiful St. Lucia! It's just under 3,000 feet high, and so straight up out of the sea.

Views from up high are ecstatic. They change the depth and width of how you see everything. The limitless sky above makes you feel free and unencumbered.

It's not how high the mountain is — the challenge is to climb as far as you are led; experience all that it has to offer both on the way up and back down again.

Knock Knock

I long for what I cannot touch

and ache for what I cannot have

But in my soul lies a fullness—

loving you

There's laughter in freedom of thought

and movement expressed

through words...

words like gold nuggets overflowing

from a treasure chest...

words pouring through

my fingertips searching for answers,

perhaps searching for more love...

Knock, knock...are you there?

...a hollowed response – reflecting emptiness...

and so...I long for what I cannot touch and

celebrate what my heart does have

October 16, 2003

Exasperating when we can't have what we long for. It feels lonely to want, to knock, to ask and hear an echo — your own.

Where do we go when we feel desperate to hear something, anything...well, not really.

In the end, we will hear an answer right where we are. It does take a shift in focus: recall the half-full/half-empty glass question.

Find that memory, hope, or feeling which you can harness and celebrate. Whether individually or in partnership, wouldn't it be wonderful if somehow everyone could find that one thread of good and then begin weaving again?

Longing

it's as though I feel it coming...

the familiar absence and ache...

missing you though

you're not

yet gone

don't go again...

not like

before

i'm looking for some place

to hide from what 'that' will

feel like

but where do i run

when it's all inside...

to feel saddened in the

midst of happiness,

lonely whilst reveling in joy

they say it's not being

present to be "here" and

"there" too

i'm everywhere...

loving, longing

and overflowing

in one ecstatic

inhaling breath

and sighing for the

escaping, exhaling

lost moment

where do i belong?

perhaps somewhere

in between

as my heart inhales

slowly, fully

and

my head says

"let the breath go"

is this not the

rhythm of life?

one part yielding

to its 'other'

to flow, to hold

is to live and love

until the last breath

… the last longing…

November 23, 2006

Love Letter

Night,

through the beauty of your blackness,

surrounded by diamonds in your sky

I shine and feel good

in the expansiveness

of your space,

Moon

April 6, 2003

Everything is in relationship with everything else. Do we really think that the moon does not love and appreciate the night? Can you imagine how it would look, would feel without it? And the night, think of the gratitude it must hold for the moon in all her phases and moods. Sometimes it seems to swallow her up in a possessive embrace.

To become aware of the relationships existing all around us, regardless of us, is to love, respect and cherish all that is....

How Do I Hold You?

I hold you

in my heart...

behind closed eyes

I watch you

move and smile

my heart

has memorized you

that is how

I'll hold you

I hold you

in my thoughts

my body remembers

the choreograph

of our dance

it is one

only we

can create...

and there too,

I hold you...

I wrap myself

in and around

your written

and spoken words,

they teach,

they touch

and reach deeply

into my soul

where ...

I hold you...

August 4, 2004

What a lovely, open-ended question to ask or be asked?

We can answer it in so many ways, unique to whom you are asking and who you are to them. The question is an invitation to express love, appreciation, sorrow, growth — it could open floodgates. It begs for an expansive, thoughtful response.

It may come full of surprises. Try it with family members, friends and lovers: "How do I hold you?"

Moon Rocks

white in the night

against the silent

darkness

the moon rocks

bright its light,

my heart nestles

in the curves

as the moon rocks

enticing, inviting

I gaze, I laze

in the rhythm

of the moon's rock

gently swaying

back and forth

I rest

as the moon rocks

it changes ever,

ever so slowly

timed

to perfection

I bounce,

I laugh

I lay

as the moon rocks

January 18, 2002

I'm driving home one night here in the States. On a dark stretch of the road I look up and notice the moon!

I saw a rocking chair in the dark sky and the jazz of Moon Rocks began dancing in my head.

A smile, a memory, warmth or appreciation is just a glance away. Look up, out, from where you are, right now, is there something there for you to be grateful for? In nature, it is always free.

Soak it all in…make a love prayer/song out of the natural beauty that surrounds us.

Together

Far beyond our earth:

invisible places

where we meet

and touch

each other...

Apart

Together

Apart...

Together again

In natural hours of separation

we smile

alone

with others...

Together we move

through space,

filled with love and learning

We fly,

circling round...

exploring life's

mysterious wonders...

you land,

I land

Apart...

Together

How else do you explain that we live our lives on different planes — if you think I'd just been watching a Superman episode, at least you'll have the gist of the possibilities? Then think dream state, and that takes you closer yet.

We have experiences, at night during sleep, which we may not remember in the morning. Or if we can, we simply don't find the language to describe it.

But...you just know that you've been somewhere... sometimes living out a fantasy, sometimes participating in a secret, yet sacred, rendezvous.

Energy, especially motivated by love, is more powerful and faster than Superman or the famed speeding bullet! When we get it — really understanding the combination of love and thought — we stand back totally awed by its fruit.

Gratitude Whispers

breathing deep whispers

of gratitude for love

I lie here

contemplating

sacred thoughts of you

thoughts which fill my body,

my soul...

a passion so moving

...an intensity so strong...

I melt,

surrendering like

timber engulfed in flame

softly, gently putting out

the fires of desire...

breathing deeply

I sigh in gratitude...in love

you

how is it that I think of you

as naturally as rain is falling down...

down into my sunset...

and as it rises into my east...

into the flickering flames of

silent moments—

soft sounds of you—

over the roar of my own thoughts

there you are

how is it that...

March 26, 2003

Night & Day

Warming my body with his golden

rays of love,

showering me with

gifts of life

and light...

Oh happy, happy day

Soothing my soul with moonfuls

of radiating,

pulsating energy:

my night fills me

his hands rest me

as they perfect me...

Oh silent, sacred night

Loving day...

and

loving night

he ignites me

he inspires me

and

I am

Whole

November 24, 2002

Have you ever felt that there are two, or more, distinct parts of you yearning for attention?

That's what Night & Day describes. In a literal sense, we love our nights and days for the important part each plays in our lives.

We sometimes discover later in the 'day' who we really are. And that what we need changes with time. It requires a lot of courage and love to acknowledge the realization.

And when or if you do, you recognize, gratefully, that it is all good.

Another Horizon

trees swaying

inviting me as

I leap closer

and closer...

the water beckons

I keep walking---

blue, green, dark, wet

methodic movement whilst

the sea gulls soar above me

and the ocean's life

perpetuates itself below...

dancing forward

I step over the edge...

beyond sight

...and I joyfully

start all over

again

July 14, 2002

Nature assists us even as we move toward our death, our transition to the greater journey beyond.

In a sense we are always on our way 'there' — from the time we are born, we weave and wind our way slowly toward the life beyond the one we are living.

I was looking out onto Labrellote Bay in St. Lucia when I wrote these thoughts. The bay was calm, inviting and provided a peaceful backdrop upon which to walk on water…and, when the time comes, right on out of here…

A Master of Disguise

I see you through the skylight,

through the trees,

bright, white

bold, proud...

so full of mystery

an attractive pull,

you draw me

to stare, to search

for your light, your love

Sometimes you hide from me

behind a mist of movement

and take on a color shrouded

as if by a dark cloak

and then, just when I'm

totally taken by your

beauty, your awe...

you change again like magic

A sliver here, a little more there

you meet me half-way,

in the darkness

I still know it's you

your beauty always

mesmerizes me...

Oh Master of Disguise

August 24, 2002

Sacred Ties

softly bind us together

gently keep us as one...

united in our understanding

of each other

sacred ties

of joy...

the ordinary,

the magical,

deepest sadness

and back again

every moment

holds you...

as you embrace mine

and we share

the one thought...

that sacred tie

called

Love

March 1, 2005

Stars At Life

jewels illuminate

and orchestrate

the night

within a symphony of

light and love

delicately arranged by the

Maestro who knows,

who conducts and inspires

us to take note

and play well

this greatest instrument,

...this life

October 19, 2002

Autumn...time...

shades of jade

now hues of

golden red

and

blazing orange...

stately in your beauty...

swaying proudly

though your robe

of wonder

slowly

drops

away

I love you now...

and will love you

during death's cold

interval

when we're both

alone,

until we meet again

and spring delivers

you back to me

vibrant,

alive...

pulsating with life

and so

we go on...

in time

November 13, 2002

Beyond

I struggle...

daily...

to move beyond,

behind

the smaller me

the me most

people see to

Me

most would hardly

recognize

each of us has our

"other" who is

our greatest

asset

who represents our

truest wealth

the One

who travels

through many

lifetimes

learning, yearning

to be the One

who speaks,

listens

who longs to just be

the One

move on beyond me

June 15, 2005

The Mirror Holders

open your eyes

when a mirror holder

shows you

your own face

and heart

helping you feel

and finally

reveal

your very own soul

be ready to hear

though

the mirror holder

does not speak

for he has no intentions

other than

this divine task

she requires nothing

other than

to be steady

and steadfast

...so be still

when stillness

requires

your attention

they may not even

know you

except during the

brief moments it takes

to reflect

you to yourself

so...be grateful...

for time

which may not

always be

measurable

move if a mirror holder

beckons forward,

for it is really

you

following your own

chosen path...

and hold your mirror

when it is handed

to you...

it is time...

June 15, 2005

Time for what? Time to do it yourself! Life gets us to a point where it pushes us out there all by ourselves. It is your time now: no more handholding, no more reflecting — time to sink, swim or climb. Often it takes all three.

The Gift

In my father's dreams

Africa loomed large

And so, as he made his dream

Our reality,

I came to view my world

Through the eyes of Africa

As a child, I saw only its beauty,

Learned to value

The aesthetic of its cultures and shared my

father's vision of

Africa's enormous expanse

and possibilities

He served God through the Africa

He loved

My father imparted many lessons

And values from which I have grown...

But the gift I most treasure was the gift of his dreams...

And for that, I am truly grateful.

September 28, 2001

Love is a Mountain

My body, mind and my soul are

already there

Love is my mountain and I will move

through her layers, savoring mystical

moments...and I will climb...

I will climb to the peaks and soar

in love's majestic ecstasy

and there I will know

that love really is a mountain to share

Spilling over with joy...

cascading down

like a waterfall...

my mountain and I are one...

Love is a mountain

I climb

September 1, 2003

Mountains come with their own personalities, conditions and environmental challenges, as well as their own qualities, opportunities and rewards. There are highs, lows, successes and disappointments, different terrains and temperatures — everything that makes up the nuances of life.

We progress through our lives as one set of experiences draws from and adds to others. We climb mountains almost every day. Some are more like little hills, others with altitudes that seem horrific.

We plan, we prepare, we pray — this, simplistically, is how to climb any mountain.

A Mountain

Mount Kilimanjaro

Our friends hosted a wonderful send off party for us. They made a three dimensional cake, a replica of Mt. Kilimanjaro! A month before we left I wrote a journal entry which reflected thoughts and some reactions to the Perry sisters' "epic journey." My favorite is still what an older southern relative said to Mother: "They must not have anything else to do."

We wanted to have fun, be safe, and we really, really wanted to make it to the top! I wanted to go because of inspired memories combined with turning fifty and wanting to do something significant with my sisters. In my journaling, I acknowledged that if we did not get to the peak, we still would have had a successful journey.

I could not possibly have defined what a "successful journey" entailed. How was I to know what adventures lay ahead, what fears we would each have to face, surrender, or overcome. We had prepared by exercising our leg muscles and practicing on a small mountain in Maryland called Sugar Loaf — a minute fraction of what Kilimanjaro held in altitude. I learned that it is hard, if not impossible to practice ahead of time on any of life's mountains and pathways. There is only one Kilimanjaro. In the end, you simply put on your boots, if you have them, and start moving when it's time to go.

Kilimanjaro was indeed a mountain of experiences. It reminds me of a quote from author, Marianne Williamson: "Our deepest fear is not that we are inadequate. Our deepest fear is that we are powerful beyond measure. It is our light, not our darkness that frightens us. As we are liberated from our own fears our presence automatically liberates others."

The impact our trip had on others as we were actually experiencing it was amazing. From start to finish many shared stories of how they would support and be with us as we journeyed our way over, up and through.

This was Kat's and Shirley's first trip back to East Africa in thirty-one years. All our friends and family were on board in celebration of our journey — everyone knew what it meant to us, to return home.

The night before we began, I woke up around 1:30 a.m. with thoughts about what it really took to climb a five-day expedition up this or any mountain. The answer came wrapped up in a wordy, holistic paradigm, but its essence was clear: be present, stay focused.

In spite of this clarifying message, I moved through each day struggling to keep my focus; often concerned whether I could face tomorrow's mountain.

Our mountain experience moved us through rainforests, alpine meadows and semi-desert terrain; through a scorching sun and wintry nights. And, as we ascended, we climbed through corresponding layers of physical, emotional, mental and spiritual levels too.

Here is a rendition of what happened:

On Day 1 we had a slow climb to the 9,000 feet mark, just over 3,000 feet from our base altitude. The rainforest was just exquisite, hushed, except for the periodic sounds of waterfalls and monkeys swinging through trees. I swear some of them were laughing at us! We reached Mandara Hut after travelling a little over four hours. It was very campy, but adequate (after a three-day excursion in the Niger desert five years before; almost anything qualified as adequate).

On Day 2 we moved to 12,500 feet reaching Horombo Hut after an exhausting, tedious trek. It took us eight hours going up little hills, down little valleys and up little hills, down little valleys. That is when I discovered that mountains aren't all up hill and that you get to coast once in a while!

It really should not have taken us quite that long. We moved so slowly because my sister Kat started having problems — in her own words, she had "no power." She suffered from altitude sickness, a common problem with mountain climbers. That night, Kat decided she would turn back in the morning so that Shirley and I could continue. We had made that decision earlier just in case one of us became unable to move on.

The next morning, however, she felt better, perkier and thought she would test herself on the next leg; we happily agreed.

It was a great morning. We woke up to an exquisite treat: we were above the clouds, looking down at "white fluffy pillows" below us! It was exhilarating — being above the clouds — only planes do that. We started with such dramatic beauty, however, Day 3 had a rather traumatic end.

We were well into the high desert, a flat area known as the *saddle*. We hadn't expected desert terrain on a mountain. Yet, Kili's top was looming so very close, not quite touchable. We acknowledged much too late in the day though, that Kat could not make it to Kibo — our next site. We had already hiked over 6 hours and there were at least two more hours to Kibo given our pace.

So, after an emotional, yet easy decision to turn around at just over 14,500 feet, we began to laboriously retrace our steps, until help finally arrived. We were tense because dusk was setting in. We had asked other climbers and their guides, both going up to Kibo and down to Horombo to request an emergency crew for us.

Although desperately hopeful, we were not absolutely certain when or if a stretcher was coming. It finally did —up over the hill, six men ran down toward us. I almost cried with relief.

The team took Kat back to Horombo. Shirley, our guide and I made it safely through pitch-blackness other than the one flashlight which we found in Kat's backpack. We weren't expecting to use flashlights until later that night...hers "should have, could have been" where ours were —with the porters who had carried our things on to Kibo. Thankfully, there was light.

We monitored Kat throughout the night, keeping her fluids up. The rescue workers were ready at any time to take her back to the mountain's base should the need arise before dawn.

We made it through another shivery night. Given Kat's

condition, we were scared; yet spoke encouraging words to each other through frozen breaths searching for oxygen.

We were relieved to see dawn arrive. In the early morning, the rescue workers took her down the mountain for the final stretch. Shirley and I did not accompany her as the rescue team executes a rapid descent; we could not possibly have kept up.

It took us another seven hours to get back to the base — we enjoyed every minute of it. The view down is so different from the view one sees going up—same mountain, another perspective, and we were ready for it.

Had events unfolded the way they were supposed to we would have woken up at midnight (the end of Day 3) to begin our final ascent for a steep, six hour climb up the *scree* (possibly a short form of scream?!) in well below zero degrees, to Gillman's Point at 18,635 feet. The estimated arrival time was 6:00 a.m. on Day 4 — with the promise of a "fiery sunrise from behind Mawenzi." Reaching Uhuru Peak (most climbers do not go any farther than Gillman's) at just over 19,300 feet, is for some, icing on the cake!

Well, that did not happen. However, we did climb to 'our mountain top.' During the moments after deciding to turn back, I felt strangely complete. After all, we had reached way up the mountain, though not to its highest peaks. Sometimes we are so busy trying to get to the top that we do not fully appreciate the altitudes and views that we do attain. I actually felt both a release and a relief from facing the unknowns of the final ascent. I admit there was a marked degree of fear surrounding going up and coming down the *scree*. I walked away comfortable with the fact that on this go around the very, very top just was not to be.

There are so many details of a journey such as this. What did we eat? What about potty stops?! Breathing was a challenge too. However, it is amazing how one can consciously direct one's body to adjust to new rhythms.

I also didn't mention that I audibly called the names of many of our friends, keenly aware of their 'presence', especially on Day 3 when we walked through the clouds. It was quite a fascinating experience. The mist of the clouds was cooling and a reprieve from the hot sun. It was an amazing sensation representing, to me, the thoughts of those who were energetically with our every step. Some of my friends later shared how they were with us in some rather creative, yet tangible ways.

The journey thrilled us — through all the thoughts and feelings: euphoria, confidence, despair, joy, fear, exuberance, awe and the physical climb itself.

I wrote the poem, which inspired the title of this book, Love Is A Mountain, almost a month prior to our climb. After Kili, I proudly granted myself a new title: Mozella, Mountain Climber.

It never ends. Isn't this how we move through our lives — searching for and hopefully experiencing our very own best selves?

And what we seek in ourselves, are we not on a quest to motivate others to expand as well?

Our mountains teach us so much of what we need to know. They encourage and instruct us. Ultimately, the lessons can be refined to one operative, all encompassing word: Love.

Love is the force and energy that fuels our individual and collective journeys.

Find it, explore it, share and experience it and you will have discovered the single most extraordinary power in the entire universe. It will take you up any mountain, because Love is so much more…

About The Author

Love Is a Mountain is Mozella Perry Ademiluyi's first book. A CD of selected poems from the book, read by Mozella, accompanied by specially created jazz music, is also available. Mozella's love for poetry and literature began during her East African school days. Her college years led to a life-long journey exploring paths of self- awareness.

Influenced by her extensive travels around the world, Mozella spent a decade advising and representing African artisans, designers and artists in their economic pursuit of export market opportunities abroad. During this period, she and her sisters promoted entrepreneurs -- primarily from Africa and the Caribbean -- by offering high quality merchandise through their upscale retail business, African Eye, in Washington, D.C.

An attorney, philanthropist and social entrepreneur, Mozella's passion is offering youth a foundation in holistic approaches to life skills - the essential education typically unavailable through formal schooling. She is a volunteer, and founder of a non-profit organization: Rising Sun Cultural and Educational Programs. The organization educates, entertains and inspires youth through its unique signature programs: The Wealth Club and Culture Connection. The former program defines wealth as a balance of physical, intellectual, spiritual, emotional and financial well-being.

Mozella is married, has three sons and several other adult children to whom she is mom. The family calls several places in the world home.

Mozella offers a poetic perspective to individuals on a path of transformation and self-discovery. She is available as a creative speaker and workshop leader.

Mozella invites you on one of her upcoming Soul Journeys which will include: Machu Picchu (Peru) Atlas Mountains (Morocco) and a return to Mount Kilimanjaro (Tanzania).

For further information, please visit
www.loveisamountain.com

Contact:

Mozella Perry Ademiluyi
Love Is A Mountain, LLC
4800 Hampden Lane
Suite 200
Bethesda, MD 20814

Email: info@loveisamountain.com

CPSIA information can be obtained at www.ICGtesting.com
Printed in the USA
BVOW011241030612

291606BV00003B/1/P